SUSPECTED POEMS

SUSPECTED POEMS

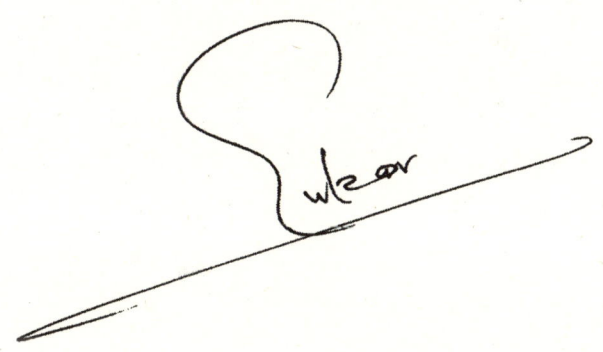

TRANSLATED BY
PAVAN K. VARMA

PENGUIN

VIKING

VIKING

USA | Canada | UK | Ireland | Australia
New Zealand | India | South Africa | China | Singapore

Viking is part of the Penguin Random House group of companies
whose addresses can be found at global.penguinrandomhouse.com

Published by Penguin Random House India Pvt. Ltd
4th Floor, Capital Tower 1, MG Road,
Gurugram 122 002, Haryana, India

Penguin
Random House
India

First published in Viking by Penguin Random House India 2017

Copyright © Gulzar 2017
Translation copyright © Pavan K. Varma 2017

All rights reserved

10 9 8 7 6 5 4 3 2

ISBN 9780670089611

Typeset in RequiemText by Manipal Digital Systems, Manipal
Printed at Replika Press Pvt. Ltd, India

www.penguin.co.in

MIX
Paper from
responsible sources
FSC® C016779

This is a legitimate digitally printed version of the book and therefore might not
have certain extra finishing on the cover.

To
Govind,
Meghna
and Samay

for the promised times

Contents

Contents

Foreword

कुछ मजबूरी हो गई है, कि दिन अख़बार ही से शुरू होता है।

पहला सफ़हा, ख़ास तौर पर दहशतनाक ख़बरों से भरा होता है, और पढ़ते हुए depression शुरू हो जाता है। दूसरे पर कुछ ख़ास नहीं होता। तीसरे सफ़हे पर Obituary, यानी उन लोगों की तस्वीरें जो मर गये हैं। ज़्यादातर सभी मुस्कुराती हुई तस्वीरें होती हैं। बल्कि कुछ-कुछ हंसती हुई। हमेशा लगता है, हंस के पूछ रहे हैं:

'कब आओगे? अभी तक ज़िंदा हो?'

चौथे, पांचवें सफ़हे पर कुछ इश्तेहार और कुछ छोटी-छोटी शहर भर की ख़बरें और फिर स्यास्तदानों के बयान शुरू हो जाते हैं। लम्बे-लम्बे—जी.टी. रोड से भी लम्बे! और उसके बाद, रोज़मर्रा के बयान, और उन पर चर्चे और तबसरे।

चाय के कप में सुबह का पहला रस्क डुबोते-डुबोते आपको भी 'टिप्पणियां' सूझने लगती हैं। आख़िर रोज़मर्रा का मामला है। जो आप ज़ेरेलब कहते हैं। वो खुलकर नहीं कह सकते। वरना 'धरे' जायेंगे। कोई कान लगा कर सुन ले, तो कान मरोड़ दे।

'क्या कह रहे हो?'

और आप अनुपम खेर की तरह कह रहे होंगे:

    'मेरा वो मतलब नहीं था!'

लेकिन आपने जो भी कहा, वो शक की नज़र से देखा जायेगा। ये सब वही 'मशकूक' नज़्में हैं जिन्हें *Suspected Poems* का नाम दे दिया है। उर्दू में होता तो 'मशकूक नज़्में' कहता।

Translator's Note

Gulzar Sahib writes poetry of an order that has few parallels today. His poems are, therefore, hardly 'suspect'! So when he told me that the next volume of his poems would be called *Suspected Poems*, I was both amused and intrigued.

By now, along a remarkably rewarding journey, I have translated three other volumes of Gulzar's poems—*Selected Poems, Neglected Poems* and *Green Poems*. But, this is the first time I have worked on a collection that is 'suspected'!

As always, there is a method to Gulzar's occasionally elliptical genius. To my mind, these poems are all part of a specific genre. That genre relates both to larger public issues and to politics. It is not as though Gulzar has not poetically commented on developments in this area in the past. But, for the first time perhaps, all the poems in a volume by him are organically animated by this theme.

It would be devaluing Gulzar's poetic sophistication to believe that he might pen a polemical or partisan lyric on issues of national concern. His style, as always, is to allude, to evoke, to suggest, to provoke and to prod a process of thought through irony, understatement and humour. He will make an indication, signal to a certain direction, and leave the reader to draw his or her own conclusion. Or, he will make a point whose inference is clear, but the language is deliberately ambivalent, in order to only further reinforce the point he wishes to make.

The poems in this collection may be titled as 'suspected', but they are, as with all of Gulzar's writings, exceptionally powerful, and as importantly, highly relevant to what is happening in the public space today. Collectively, they constitute a carefully crafted commentary that is a subtle but definitive evaluation of some aspects of our evolving republic. The purpose of the poems is to compel the reader towards introspection. The journey, as always, is inward, even if the issues of his poetic survey are external. In the cacophonous world we live in, they are a fine example of how a point can be made with anguish and concern, but without malice or acrimony.

I have greatly enjoyed translating these 'suspected' poems. Given their content and treatment, they provide, in their intensity, style and brevity, another kind of experience for a translator.

As I have said before, Gulzar Sahib is a meticulous linguistic craftsman. His lyrics create rapturous fans, but a somewhat harried translator! Harried—not only because of the beauty of the original that he must try and capture, but also because the density of the imagery and idioms employed. Translating Gulzar is always a pleasure and a challenge. I have done my best, but if there is anything lacking in the translation, I crave forgiveness. I would also like to say a big thank you to Udayan Mitra of Penguin Random House, who edited the manuscript and so elegantly made up for some of my own shortcomings.

The real reward of working with Gulzar Sahib is the interactions you have with him as part of the process. I greatly treasure my personal friendship with him, and I can only wish him many more decades of creative writing.

Pavan K. Varma

SUSPECTED
POEMS

नई दिल्ली में वैसे तो नया कुछ भी नहीं है . . .

नई दिल्ली में वैसे तो नया कुछ भी नहीं है
मगर हर पांच सालों में नई सरकार आती है
पुराने मसले लेकर, नये मनसूबे करते हैं
मियानें खींच कर फिर से . . .
वो ज़ंग आलूदा सब क़ानून फिर से आज़माते हैं
कि जिन से घास कटती है, न गर्दन!

There's Nothing New
in New Delhi

There is nothing really new in New Delhi
Except that every five years a new government comes in
And converts old issues to new schemes.
Opening scabbards anew
They unsheathe again all the rusted laws
That can cut neither grass, nor necks!

वतन की बात करें!

ज़रा सा आओ ना बैठो, वतन की बात करें
उम्मीदें डूब गईं जो निगल-निगल के भंवर
उम्मीदें, हांफ रही हैं जो बादबानों में
उम्मीद-औ-शौक़ के क़त्ल-औ-ग़बन की बात करें . . .?

गुज़श्ता सालों में ऐसा नहीं कि कुछ न हुआ
गुज़श्ता सालों में लेकिन . . .
फ़लक खुला तो गिरी धूप, जैसे गर्द गिरे
हर एक रोज़ फ़लक पोंछा, उठके साफ़ किया

हमारे टख़नों पे कुल्हाड़ियां गिरीं लेकिन
लहू-लुहान क़दम, सीढ़ियों पे चढ़ते रहे
निकल तो आये हैं, हम घुटनों-घुटनों दलदल से

Shall We Talk about the Country?

Come sit down for a moment, let's talk about
our country:
Hopes that drowned in whirlpools again and again
Hopes, panting like wind in the sails
Hopes and wants, murdered and looted
Shall we talk about them again?

It's not that nothing was achieved in the past
But in the years of yore
Whenever the sky cleared the sun shone down
Like a shower of dust;
Every day we rose to dust the sky, trying to
make it clean.

Axes hit us on our ankles but still
We kept climbing the steps with blood-soaked feet
We may have emerged from the quicksand that
was knee-deep

अभी खुला नहीं . . . कैसे चमन की बात करें

चलो ना . . . चलते चलें . . . और वतन की बात करें . . .!

But how can we talk of a paradise
That is not yet in sight?

So come, let's keep walking, and talk about our country!

26 जनवरी!

कार सिगनल पे रुकी जैसे ही, वो दौड़ा फिर से
'पोलियो' मारी हुई, टांग पे ता-थैया करता!

मां ने रोका भी मगर . . . खांसी ने कहने न दिया
'दो रूपये का है तिरंगा बाबू . . . ''पब्लिक डे'' है
देश का अच्छा बनेगा . . . ले लो सेठ!'

तभी सिगनल बदला—और कार गई!
देश की झांकी में इक बार कभी ये भी दिखाया जाये!

26th January

The moment the car stopped at the signal,
off he went again,
Hobbling along on his polio-afflicted leg.

His mother tried to stop him
But her cough smothered her voice.
'Two rupees for this tricolour, it's Public Day
Take one Seth, good for the country.'

The signal changed, and the car moved on.
Perhaps this scene can also figure
Somewhere in the festive pageants of our nation!

ये ताज़ा ख़बरें . . .

ये ताज़ा ख़बरें, जो ताज़ा हैं, आज के लिये हैं
हरी-हरी सब्ज़ ताज़ा तर्कारियां हैं सारी
ये आज ही इस्तमाल कर के, भूल जायें!

ख़बर है 'डौड़ा' ज़िला में आतंकवादियों ने
अठारह लोगों को जो गडरिये थे और पहाड़ी पे अपनी
भेड़ें चरा रहे थे
पकड़ के सब को
इकट्ठा कर के
उड़ा के गोली से धूप में लाशें डाल दी हैं
जहाँ पे सूरजमुखी के फूलों की कियारियाँ थीं

पचास सालों से हो रहा है . . .
ये फिर हुआ है
कि जैसे कल्ले में वक़्त ने पान रख लिया है
चबा रहा है . . .!

'उड़ीसा' में फिर से एक सैलाब की वजह से पचास गाँव

This Latest News

This latest news is news only for today
Like fresh green vegetables
That must be consumed today, or forgotten.

The news is that terrorists in district Daudha
Caught eighteen shepherds who were
Tending to their sheep in the mountains
Herded them together
Shot them dead
And left their corpses in the sun
Where the sunflowers blossomed.

It has been happening for fifty years—
It has happened again!
As though time has put a paan in his mouth
And continues to chew it!

In Odisha, due to floods, fifty villages

जो आधे डूबे हुए हैं पानी में,
मुल्क से कट चुके हैं नौ दिन गुज़र गये हैं

गले-गले तक लपकता पानी . . .
सरों पे बर्तन या बच्चा, जो भी ज़रूरी समझा
उठा के कुछ लोग ऊँची जगहों पे मुन्तक़िल होते जा रहे हैं
कि पानी चढ़ता ही जा रहा है
छतों पे बूढ़े ज़ईफ़ बैठे हैं, सर पे मंडलाते, गिद्ध चीलें हटा रहे हैं

ये दो बरस पहले भी हुआ था
ये दस बरस पहले भी हुआ था
ग़रीबी जितनी पुरानी हैं ये तमाम ख़बरें

ये ताज़ा तस्वीरें तब भी देखी थीं, जब कोई कैमरा नहीं था
ये ताज़ा ख़बरें . . .!

Are once again drowned under water
Cut off from the rest of the country for nine days;
Surging waters rising up to the necks
People carrying a child or utensils on their heads
—Whatever is considered essential—
Are moving to higher ground
Even as the water continues to rise;
The aged and sick sit on roofs
Trying to keep away the vultures
Hovering above their heads . . .

This happened two years ago
This happened ten years ago as well
All these stories are as old as poverty itself.

These 'new' pictures we saw even then
When there was no camera
This latest news
Must be consumed today, and forgotten.

अख़बार

अख़बार उठाया तो कुछ छोटी-छोटी ख़बरें, गोद में आन गिरीं!

'डस्टबिन' में फेंके हुये इक बच्चे को
इक कुतिया ने तीन दिन तक दूध पिला कर ज़िन्दा रखा
फिर लोग ले गये . . .
दिन रात वहीं, पंजों से अब वो कूड़ा कुरेदा करती है!

'पासपोर्ट' कमिशनर ने दरख़्वास्त से सर उठा कर पूछाः
'कोई तिल? या मस्सा कोई तेरे बदन पर?
जन्म निशानी कोई? . . .
कोई निशान जो मिट न सके?'
चंद मिन्ट कुछ सोचा, फिर सरदार ने यकदम शर्ट उतारीः
'आग का एक निशान है, सर जी,
चौरासी का!
ये मिट नहीं सकता!'

Newspaper

As I took up the newspaper
Some small, insignificant stories fell into my lap.

A child, thrown into a dustbin
Was kept alive
By a dog who suckled him for three days;
Then, some people came and took the child away.
The dog now paws at the garbage day and night . . .

The Passport Commissioner looked up
From the application before him and said:
'Any mole or wart on your body?
Any birthmark?
Any identification that cannot be erased?'

The Sikh thought for a few minutes
And then suddenly took off his shirt:
'There is a burn mark, Sirji,
From '84.
This can't be erased!'

रोज़ वही अख़बार का कॉलम!

रोज़ वही अख़बार का कॉलम
घूंट कसीली ख़बरों के
रोज़ वही वादों के लुक़मे
काट के जुमले, लफ़्ज़ लफ़्ज़ निगलते रहना

कितनी देर चबाये कोई
'च्युंगगम' रोज़ बयानों के
अब तो ये मामूल हुआ है
थूक दो मुंह भर जाये तो

वरना ज़र्दा डाल के पान की पीक उड़ाओ
ख़ूशबूदार क़िमाम लगा के, वक़्त निगलते जाओ!

The Same News

Every day the same newspaper column
Gulps of the same brackish news
Every day the same mouthful of promises
Sentences dissected
Each word chewed again and again.

How long can one munch
The chewing gum of daily statements?
Now one has come to learn:
Just spit it out
If the mouth can take no more.

Or else, add some *zarda*
To a betel leaf
And quaff the paan around
With some aromatic *qimam* put on it—
Just keep on swallowing time!

गुमशुदा

तलाश है एक गुमशुदा की
पचास पचपन की उम्र होगी
उड़ा-उड़ा रंग ज़र्दी मायेल
उदास आँखें हैं, ख़ुश्क रहती हैं बेशतर वो
भवें कई बार आग में जल चुकी हैं उसकी
उठाये रखता था पलकों पर जलते ख़्वाब हमेशा
मेरा पड़ोसी था, हमसफ़र था . . .

वो आधे रसते तलक मेरे साथ-साथ ही था
फिर उसका क़द धीरे-धीरे कम होने लग गया था
वो दूर तक जो उफ़क़ नज़र आते थे वो धुंधलाने लग गये थे
नज़र से उम्मीद की चमक भी उतर रही थी
दिलासे देकर
कभी-कभी उसको कन्धों पर ले के भी चला, पर . . .
वो अपने पैरों पे चलने की ज़िद न छोड़ता था

Searching for a Missing Man

Searching for a missing man
Aged about fifty or fifty-five
Pallid, of yellowish-pale complexion
Sad eyes, for the most part dry
The eyebrows singed many times in the past
The eyelashes always holding aloft a blaze
of dreams
He was my neighbour, my fellow traveller.

Half the way he travelled with me
Then, his stature slowly started shrinking
The horizons began to blur in his sight
The gleam of hope dimmed in his eyes;
Consoling him
Sometimes I even carried him on my shoulders
But he was obstinate, he wanted to walk on his own.

कलाई मेरी ग्रिफ़्त से छुट गई है उसकी
वो शहर के इस हुजूम में गुम हो गया है
तलाश है आम आदमी की
तलाश है मुझको गुमशुदा की!

His hand has slipped from my grasp
He is lost in the multitudes of this town
The search is on for the common man
A search for a person missing!

ट्रेफ़िक जैम!

सत्तर साल हुए हैं, मैं इस ट्रेफ़िक जैम में फँसा हुआ हूँ
न्यु देहली की पार्लियामेंट रोड पे होड़ लगी है
दायें तरफ़ की एक क़तार में धक्कम पेल लगी है कब से
बायें तरफ़ कुछ और क़तारें उलझ गई हैं
देखो तो बन्दे पर बन्दा चढ़ा हुआ है
सीटें बांट रहा है कोई, कुर्सियाँ खींच रहा है
न आगे बढ़ता है कोई, न पीछे हटता है
ट्रेफ़िक जैम में फसाँ हुआ हूँ
सत्तर साल हुए हैं!

Traffic Jam

For seventy years I am caught in a traffic jam
A great rush is on at New Delhi's Parliament Street:
In a line to the right, people jostle and push
No one knows since when;
To the left some other lines lie entangled;
Have a look, men are standing, one upon another:
Somebody is distributing seats, another is pulling
chairs away;
No one moves ahead, or steps aside.
I am caught in a traffic jam
For the last seventy years!

Use the Diversion!

वो हिन्दू थे सुना है . . .!
बस इक दिन यूं ही जब अपनी गली के मोड़ पर आये
जहां पे रास्ता खोदा हुआ था
वहां दंगे लगे थे, आग थी, दो तीन लाशें थीं
वो खड्ढा उनके खूं से भर गया था
वहीं इक बोर्ड पर लिखा हुआ था
Work in Progress—use the diversion.

मुसलमां हो गये वो!
मगर खड्ढे का खूं सूखा नहीं अब तक
सड़क पे काम जारी है!

Use the Diversion

He was a Hindu, I was told.
One day, when he turned
The corner of his street
Where a pothole had been dug up
He found a riot was on.
Two–three dead bodies, flames all around,
The hole had filled up with their blood.
Next to the hole, a board proclaimed:
'Work in progress, use the diversion'.

He became a Muslim
But the blood in the pothole has not dried up
Work on the road is still in progress.

हवा बदली हुई है!

हवा बदली हुई है . . .
नज़र बदली है लोगों की
हवा में बाहें लहराने लगी हैं
छतों पर, टीन के मुर्गों को मत देखो
सड़क पर गर्दनें लोगों की देखो घूम रही हैं
हवा का रुख़ बदलने लग गया है
नये झन्डे नज़र आने लगे हैं

यही होता है झन्डे फड़फड़ाते हैं हवा में जब
हवा भी फड़फड़ाने लगती है झन्डा पकड़ कर!

The Wind Has Changed

The wind has changed
There is a change in the vision of the people
Fists are waving in the wind;
Don't look at the weathercocks on roofs
See how people's necks are turning on the streets
The wind is blowing in a new direction
New flags have started appearing.

That's what happens when flags flutter in the wind—
The wind too flutters, clasping the flag!

ये गूंगा है कौन? . . .

ये गूंगा है कौन? . . .
खांस्ता है तो लफ़्ज़ उड़ते हैं, उसके मुंह से
कि शहर को साफ़ रखना दुश्वार हो गया है
चौराहे पर बात चल रही है
लिखारी होगा—अदीब कोई
किसी ने पूछी थी उसकी राय
और . . . ज़बां काट ली थी उसकी!

Who Is This Dumb Person?

Who is this dumb person?
When he coughs, words fly around from his mouth
It has become difficult to keep the town clean;
At the town square people are talking:
Maybe a writer, perhaps some intellectual
Someone had asked him for his views
And then cut off his tongue!

कुलबर्गी . . .

मरा नहीं वो . . .
वो और था कोई जो मरा है
वहीं पे दहलीज़ पर पड़ा है

किसी ने घन्टी बजायी घर की
वो अपने बच्चों को
क, ख, ज, झ, सिखा रहा था
उठा, गया, कुन्डी खोली घर की . . .
और एक आवाज़ गूंजी, गोली की, आसमां में
'विचार' था उसके सर में कोई
जो बोलता था . . .
'विचार' दहलीज़ पर पड़ा है!

Kalburgi

He did not die . . .
The person who died and lies on the threshold
Is someone else.

Somebody rang the bell of his house;
He was teaching his children
How to write *ka, kha, ja, jha*;
He got up, went and opened the door
And there was the sound of a bullet
Reverberating in the sky.

There was a belief in his head
Which had a voice;
That belief is now lying inert on the threshold.

अल्लामा को कोई ख़बर कर दे!

ज़रा 'अल्लामा'* को कोई ख़बर कर दे
कि जिन खेतों से दहक़ां को मय्यस्सर न हुई रोटी
किसी ने खेत में जाकर जलाया ही नहीं
गंदम के ख़ोशों को . . .
कहीं कोई नहीं उट्ठा, न कोई इन्क़लाब आया!

जनाज़े उठ रहे हैं गांव-गांव से
ये सब के सब जनाज़े हैं किसानों के
जिन्होंने क़र्ज़ की मिट्टी चबा कर ख़ुदकुशी कर ली!

*जिस खेत से दहक़ां को मय्यस्सर नहीं रोटी
उस खेत के हर ख़ोशा-ए-गन्दुम को जला दो!'*

*अल्लामा मोहमद इक़बाल—उर्दू के शायर।

Inform the Alla'ma

Will someone inform the Alla'ma*
That nobody went to the fields
To burn the crop of wheat
From which a farmer could not
Even get a morsel of bread?
Nobody rose, and no cry of revolution stirred!

Funerals are taking place in every village
All of them are of farmers
Who ate the debris of debt and committed suicide!

Crops which cannot provide bread to the farmer
Burn those crops of wheat.

*Alla'ma Mohammad Iqbal, the poet.

दो लाख रूपये!

वो जिसके मरने पर, दो लाख घर वालों ने पाये हैं
उसे गर ये ख़बर होती,
कि उसकी मौत की अब इतनी क़ीमत है
तो अपने वास्ते मरता!

Two Lakh Rupees

If he knew that on his death
His family would get two lakhs
That his death is priced so high
He would have died for himself!

ये सात रंगी धनक!

ये सात रंगी धनक कौन चढ़ के साफ़ करे
हज़ार जाले लगे हैं, स्याह लगती है
कोई उम्मीद अगर उड़के छू भी ले इसको
तो गर्द उड़ती है, या रंग भुरने लगते हैं
फ़लक खुला था तो सोचा कि धूप निकलेगी
ये 'दाग़-दाग़ उजाला' भी छँट ही जायेगा
मगर इस आधी सदी में—
पुरानी छत का सा लगता है आसमान मुझे
मरीज़ लगती हैं सुबहें, ज़ईफ़ लगता है सूरज

दरख़्त इतने गिरे हैं पुराने और घने
परिन्दे डरते हैं शाख़ों पे तिनके रखते हुए
अक़ीदे तोड़े हैं इतने ज़्यादा लोगों ने
चलें जो चार क़दम, तलवे कटने लगते हैं
मैं किस उम्मीद के पर खोलूं और उड़ाऊं उसे
ये सात रंगी धनक कौन चढ़ के साफ़ करे!

फ़ैज़ अहमद फ़ैज़

The Seven-Coloured Rainbow

Who will climb up to clean this seven-coloured rainbow?
It looks black, enveloped in a thousand cobwebs.
Even if a hope can fly and touch it
Its colours will peel off, a puff of dust will rise.
When the sky opened I thought there would be sunshine
Dispelling this stain-covered* dawn
But after half a century
The sky looks like an old roof
The morning diseased, the sun aged.

So many old, dense trees have fallen
That birds fear to build a nest on the branches
People have shattered so many doctrines of faith
If we take a few steps our soles get slashed.
Which hope should unfurl its wings to fly
And clean this seven-coloured rainbow?

*Reference: Faiz Ahmed Faiz.

सेल्फ़ मेड

पुनिया के इक खेत में उसकी माँ ने थोड़ी देर
दरांती रोक के उसको जन्म दिया था
मज़दूरों ने बारी-बारी गोद में लेकर
थोड़े-थोड़े पैसों से कुछ शगुन दिया था
तभी से काम पे लगा हुआ है . . . और कमाई करता है!

भीख में अच्छे पैसे थे
हाथ पांव पे पट्टियां बाँध के
माँ मन्दिर के दरवाज़े पे रख आती थी
बाप उठा के ले आता था . . .
अपने दूध के पैसे रोज़ कमा लेता था

भीख मांग के, बीड़ी पीना सीख लिया था
होटल पर बाहर वाले की चाय लेकर
ट्रक वालों को जाकर देना . . .
पैसे, दो पैसे की चोरी वहीं पे सीखी
बाद में सीखी हाथ की सफ़ाई—

Self-made

In a field in Punia, his mother had for a moment
Kept aside her sickle to give birth to him;
One by one, the labourers took him in their lap
Gifting him, as auspicious offerings, small amounts
of money;
Ever since, he has been working, and earning too!

There was good money in begging:
With bandages tied to his hands and feet
His mother would leave him at the temple's threshold
His father would bring him back later;
He could earn enough daily to pay for his milk.

Cigarettes and snacks were paid for
By what he earned from begging;
Carrying tea for truck drivers outside the hotel
He learnt to steal paltry sums of money;
Later he learnt the real sleight of hand

चोरी चकारी तो मामूली फ़न हैं अब
हाथ सुपारी लेता है!

कानून के लम्बे हाथों के वो नाखुन काटता है
जुर्म की गंदी गलियों में, उसकी दो नालियां चलती हैं
छोटा-मोटा, डॉन-वॉन कहलाता है।

'सेल्फ़ मेड' है, कहता है!
भूल गया ये बनने में कितने लोगों के
हाथ लगे हैं
पूरे एक समाज के सिस्टम ने मिलकर ये कोशिश की
तब डॉन बना है!

Stealing and robbery were but routine talents—
Now he takes *supari*, money for killings!

He clips the nails of the long hand of the law
In the alleys of crime, his double-barrels resound
He is now a kind of small-time don.

He says, 'I am "self-made"!'
He forgets how many people contributed
To make him who he is.
The entire system of society made the effort
So he could become a don!

कफ़न

फटी चोली का ग़म भी क्यों मेरी जां?
कहीं से काट ले इक धूप का टुकड़ा
उठा ले एक पेबंद और सी ले
ज़री जैसा लगेगा
कि बन-ठन के भी आख़िर भीख ही तो मांगनी है
ग़रीबी से भला शर्मिंदगी क्या?
ग़रीबी तो हमारी सभ्यता से भी पुरानी है!

हमेशा पेट ही की फ़िक्र करती हो
बहुत जूठन मिलेगी
घाट पर सब को खिलाते हैं
वो जब मुर्दा जलाते हैं!

भला घर की परेशानी भी कैसी?
कि सर पे आसमाँ है और तकिये के लिये पीपल खड़ा है
हवा करता है बरखुर्दार, आधे चाँद की पंखी
उठा के झेलता रहता है

Shroud

My love, why must you feel bad about your torn blouse?
Just cut from somewhere a piece of sunlight
And stitch another patch to your garment
It will look like gold thread.
After all, even when dressed in all your finery
Your job is only to beg;
What is there to be ashamed of in poverty?
Poverty is older than our culture!

You are always worried about hunger;
Why worry, there will be enough leftovers
At the ghat where they serve food as ritual
When dead bodies are burnt on the pyre.

And what is the worry about a place to live?
Above your head the sky, the peepal tree your pillow
The half-moon a fan in the hands of the obedient peepal
To provide a breath of breeze . . .

तुम्हें फुटपाथ पर सोते हुये शर्मिंदगी क्यों है?
वहाँ तो पूरी इक तहज़ीब सोती है
किसी की पीठ में गट्टे नहीं पड़ते, न बल पड़ते हैं माथे पर

हमें गर फ़िक्र होती कल की, ग़म होता—
हमारा कल नहीं है
हमें औलाद थोड़ा पालना है?

वही पालेंगे भी उनको, उठायेंगे जो कूड़े से
मरे भी तो
वही हम को कफ़न देंगे
जिन्होंने जीते जी हमको हमेशा नंगा रखा है!
ग़रीबी से भला शर्मिंदगी क्या?
ग़रीबी तो हमारी सभ्यता से भी पुरानी है!

मुन्शी प्रेमचंद की 'कफ़न' कहानी के 'माधव और घेसू' के नाम!

Why do you feel ashamed to sleep on the footpath?
An entire culture sleeps there:
The backs show no knots, nor are foreheads creased.

If we had a worry for the morrow, we could be sorrowful
But we don't have a tomorrow
It's not like we have children to care for.
They will bring them up
Who pick them up from the dustbin
And even if we die
Those people
Who always kept us naked when we were alive
Will give us a shroud.

What, after all, is there to be ashamed of in poverty?
Poverty is older than our culture!

Dedicated to Madhav and Ghesu in Munshi Premchand's *Kafan.*

परिन्दे हैं या परचम?

परिन्दे हैं या परचम हैं
या काली झंडियाँ हैं
ये कव्वे शहर की बिजली की तारों पर
सभी सड़कों पे आकर भर गये हैं
किसी के जाने का मातम है या . . .
या किसी के आने पर
ये सत्याग्रह करने चले हैं!

Are These Birds or Banners?

Are these birds, or banners
Or black flags?
These crows sitting on the city's electric wires
Have come and occupied all the streets:
Are they grieving over someone passing away
Or are they on *satyagraha*
On the arrival of someone!

स्पीकर . . .

पिछले साठ मिन्ट से
बांस पे लटका एक 'स्पीकर' बोल रहा है
पूरे का पूरा मुंह खोले
मोटे-मोटे रोड़े कंकर फेंक रहा है!

एक हाथ माईक के गले में
दूसरा लोगों की गर्दन में
पेट में घुटना ठोक के कहता है: 'क्यों बच्चू?
आज तो अपनी वोटें लेकर ही जाऊँगा!'

Speaker

For the last sixty minutes
A 'speaker' hanging from a pole is bellowing
With its entire mouth open
Emitting stone sand gravel.

With one hand on the mike's throat
And the other around people's necks
He thrusts his knee into the gut, and says:
'Listen buddy, come what may,
I will not leave without my vote today!'

जलसा!

बहुत बड़ा जलसा लगता है,
जी.टी. रोड से भी लम्बी तक़रीर करेगा!
कित्ती देर से बोल रहा है, लेकिन लोग भरे जाते हैं, जैसे
बेकारों की मन्डी लगी हुई है
आलूओं की जब बोरियाँ खुलती हैं मन्डी में
यूंही लुढ़क-लुढ़क कर आलू सारे गाले भर देते हैं।

'पिछड़े वर्ग, के लोगों को आगे लाकर हम . . .'

तांगा जोतोगे क्या हम पर? . . . अमां छोड़ो . . . मर्ज़ी से सब
आगे पीछे कर लेते हो।

'आपका और ज़्यादा वक़्त न लेते हुये मैं . . .'

नहीं . . . ज़्यादा वक़्त कहाँ? आधी सदी ही गुज़री है
जब ये भाषण शुरू हुआ था

Jalsa

It seems to be a huge gathering
He will make a speech lengthier than the GT Road!
His speech has gone on endlessly
Yet people continue to pour in
A veritable *mandi* of those with nothing to do
Just like when sacks of potatoes are opened in the market
The potatoes topple over one another and fill up the yard.

'We will bring to the forefront those of the backward classes . . .'

Will you harness us to a tonga?
Forget it—
You move people in front or to the back
According to your whims.

'Not taking more of your time . . .'

Not at all, only half a century has elapsed
Since your speech began;

हिन्दोस्तान तो गन्ना है, ये छील-छील के
खाते रहो, पीढ़ी दर पीढ़ी, ख़त्म न होगा।

'मुड़ के देखें हम अपने इतिहास को लोगो . . .'

देखा था भई, गर्दन मचक गई थी मेरी
दादा परदादा तक देखा, उस से आगे
पता नहीं, हम थे कि नहीं . . .?

शाहों का ज़िक्र तो मिलता है
हम लोगों का ज़िक्र कहाँ है . . .?
नंगे बदन ही दिखते हैं शाहों को पालकी में ले जाते
आगे पीछे दौड़ते नंगे पाँव . . .
उस से पहले, उनका शिकार हुआ करता था अफ़्रीका के जंगलों में
सुना है बिक्री भी होते थे . . .
मंच पे बैठे किस इतिहास को देख रहे हो?
शायद हम दोनों के दो इतिहास हैं, दोनों अलग-अलग हैं!

'आप से वादा करते हैं हम, जितनी देर इस कुर्सी पर हैं . . .'

कुर्सी से मत उठना दोस्त, भरोसा क्या है, कौन आ बैठे
और वसीयत में भी अपनी आख़िरी ख़्वाहिश लिखकर जानाः
कुर्सी पर बिठला के चंदन की लकड़ी से चिता बनायें
दफ़न करें तो क़ब्र में भी कुर्सी लगवा के दफ़न करें!
हंसते क्या हो? तुम को क्या मालूम कि मैं क्या सोच रहा हूं?

India is like sugar cane
Keep peeling and eating it
Generations will go by
But it will not finish.

'If we look back at our history . . .'

I did look back, brother
I twisted my neck in doing so
I could see till my grandfather and great-grandfather
But beyond that, I don't know if we were there.
We find references to kings
But where are the references to the people?
Bare-bodied they carried kings in palanquins
With bare feet running around them;
Even before that they were hunted in the jungles of Africa
We hear that they were sold too . . .
Seated on the dais, what history are you talking about?
Perhaps you and I have two histories, both apart.

'We promise you, so long as we are in power . . .'

Don't ever get up from your seat of power, my friend
What's the guarantee
That someone else won't come and occupy your chair?
And in your will do write your last wish
That only after seating you on a sandalwood *kursi*
A pyre is made
And if you're buried, the *kursi* is placed in your grave!
Why do you laugh?
You have no clue what I am thinking about.

'भूख, ग़रीबी और बेकारी, जब तक ख़त्म नहीं होती हम . . .'

क्यों चिन्ता करते हो प्यारे?
हमने खुद ही कुछ न किया तो, तुम भी आख़िर . . . क्या कर लोगे? . . .
राज़ की बात तो ये है भाई! भूख लगी है।
ट्रक में भर के लाये थे जो लोग तुम्हारी पार्टी के
उन लोगों ने वादा किया था, पन्द्रह पर्सेंट काट के पूरे
एक सौ देंगे, और ऊपर से . . .
जाने दो अब! भूख लगी है, यार अब जलसा ख़त्म करो!

'So long as we do not eliminate hunger, poverty and unemployment . . .'

Why do you worry so much, my dear chap?
If we have not done anything for ourselves
What can you do?
My brother, the fact is that I am hungry!
Those from your party who packed us into a truck
Had promised that, after deducting fifteen per cent,
They will pay us a full one hundred
And, over and above that . . .
Oh, forget it!
I am hungry, let's bring this *jalsa* to an end!

बहुत से मसले लेकर गया था . . .

बहुत से मसले लेकर गया था मैं बड़े नेता की मीटिंग में
वही सब हल करेंगे
हमारी 'चाल' में पानी का प्रॉबलम है
मेरे बच्चे की फ़ीस और दाख़िले का एक मसला है
उसे दाख़िल कराने के लिये फ़न्ड देना पड़ता है
हमारी औरतें डब्बे उठाये, हाईवे के पार जाकर बैठती हैं
हमें तो शर्म आती है

बड़े नेता ने समझाया, 'करप्शन और भ्रष्टाचार से हमको
ये सिस्टम साफ़ करना है
डिमोक्रसी हमारी प्लास्टिक है, आर्टीकल नम्बर फ़ुलाना चैंज करना है
हमें जब तक हमारे हक़ नहीं मिलते
लड़ाई लड़ते रहना है!
हमारे साथ रहना तुम!'

There Were Many Problems

There were many problems I had taken
To the Leader's meeting;
He would support me to solve them.
There is the problem of water in our chawl
The payment of my child's fees
His admission to school is another issue
To admit him I have to pay money;
Our women, picking up their water canisters,
Have to cross the highway to go and squat
Frankly, we feel ashamed.

The Leader explained: 'We have to clean
The system of corruption
Our democracy is plastic
The number of some article or other has to be changed
Until we get what is our due
We have to continue the fight
You must support us!'

मैं लौट आया . . .
समझ आया नहीं कि कौन किसके मस्लों को हल करेगा!

I came back
Confused, who would solve whose problems!

ये बेमानी घास . . .

ये बेमानी घास जो पैरों में पिसती है, रौंदी जाती है
ये बेमानी, बेहिस, ढीठ है,
हर कूड़े करकट से फूटने लगती है . . .
पतली एक दरार ज़रा सी, चट्टानों में मिल जाये तो,
उगने लगती है
इस बेमानी घास में ज़िन्दा रहने की
इक ला-मतनाही ताक़त है
काट के ढेर बना के आग लगाई है
मलबे के नीचे इस को दफ़नाया है!

मारो, कूटो, क़तल करो, या फूंक दो इन को
लोगों में ज़िन्दा रहने की ला-मतनाही ताक़त होती है!

This Useless Grass

This useless grass that is squashed under our feet
And crushed
This meaningless, senseless and stubborn grass
It sprouts from any garbage or filth
And begins to grow from even the tiniest crevice it can find
In a rock.

The strength of this useless grass
Is that it has a great will to survive
It has been cut and heaped into a pile
Set on fire and buried under debris . . .

Whether you beat them, pound them
Murder them or set them on fire
People have a great will to survive.

बाबरी !

रोज़ उठते धूऐं की कालिक से
उस तरफ़ आसमां का इक टुकड़ा
सारा दिन अब सियाह रहता है
चीलें ही चीलें उड़ती रहती हैं

नीचे कुछ अधजले से पेड़ों पर
कुनबे बैठे हुए हैं गिद्धों के
पेट उभरे हुए हैं फूले हुये
कूड़े करकट की ढेरियों में अभी
ठन्डी लाशों के सर सुलगते हैं
टांगों बाहों की हड्डियों के लिये
लड़ते रहते हैं शब के चोपाये
जिसने भी पहले दाँत मारे हैं
हड्डी बोटी का हक़ उसी का है

किसने पहले कुदाल मारी थी?
हाँ यही वो ज़मीं का टुकड़ा है
कल किसी इक ख़ुदा का घर भी था!

Babri

From the smoke that rises daily
A part of the sky
Now remains black the whole day
Only pariah kites hover above.

Families of vultures sit
On some half-charred trees below
Their stomachs bloated;
Amidst the heaps of garbage lying around
Heads on ice-cold corpses smoulder
As the animals of dusk
Fight for every bone of rotting limbs
Whoever can sink their teeth in first
Has the right over that piece of flesh.

Who was the one who struck the first blow of the axe?
Yes, this indeed is that piece of land
Which till yesterday was also a home to some god!

सियासत ने, मेरे पिछवाड़े में . . .

सियासत ने,
मेरे पिछवाड़े में कुछ लोग लाकर बो दिये थे
वो सब उस मशरिक़ी बंगाल से आये थे, जिन पर
वो ज़मीन तंग हो गई थी।
हज़ारों एकड़ ज़मीं देकर . . .
अहाता खींच कर ये कह दिया थाः
'यहीं रहना!'
और कहा था, मिट्टी पानी सब मिलेगा
तुम्हारा धर्म और ज़ातें यहां महफ़ूज़ हैं सब
मगर वो रौशनी सूरज की जो तुम छोड़ आये हो
वो शायद कम मिलेगी
घटायें घेरे रहती हैं

'जो कलचर तापा करते थे . . .
चिराग़ों से उसे तुम ज़िन्दा रखना
ज़रूरत पड़ गई तो तुम अलाव भी जला सकते हो, लेकिन
यहीं से ढूंढ लेना, सूखे कीकर . . . और जला लेना!'

Politics behind My Home

Politics has gone and sown some people
Behind my home;
They have all come from East Bengal
Where there was no shelter for them.

After giving them a thousand acres
And demarcating the land, they were told:
'Stay here!
Water and land will be made available
Your religion and castes will be protected
But perhaps there will be less
Of the sunlight you had left behind.'
Clouds have hovered around them ever since.

'The culture that used to warm you
Keep that alight,' they were told,
'If necessary, light a bonfire too
But only from the dry *keekar* you find here.'

उन्हें चालिस बरस होने लगे हैं
कई नसलें उगी हैं, सूखी जंगली झाड़ियों जैसी
किसी का कृद नहीं निकला . . .
वो मिट्टी से जुड़े तो हैं,
जड़ों की उंगलियां खुलतीं नहीं उनसे
उन्हें सूरज पकड़ता है, न वो मिट्टी पकड़ते हैं!

Almost forty years have gone by
New generations have sprouted, like dry bushes
in the wild
All have remained stunted.
They are attached to the soil
But cannot put down roots
Neither can the sun catch them
Nor can they grip the soil.

कंवल के फूल

कंवल के फूल, मुझे बोधी लगते हैं सारे
सब एक रंग के चोग़े में, सब्ज़ काई पर
पद्म-आसन लगाये पानी में
न जाने किस का ध्यान करते हैं!

ये सर मुंडाये हुए बोधी बच्चे 'धर्मशाला' में
कंवल के फूलों से लगते हैं सब के सब मुझको
ये ऐसे पौधे हैं जिनकी जड़ें ज़मीं में नहीं हैं

ये उनकी नसलों से उतरे हैं सारे के सारे
जो लोग छोड़ कर अपनी जड़ें ज़मीनों में
'दलाई लामा' की हिजरत के साथ आये थे
वो लोग अपनी हवाओं से कट के जब आये
फ़लक का टुकड़ा कोई अपना काट कर नहीं लाये
सिवाये एक ख़्याली से धर्म के, क्या देते अगली नसलों को!

Lotus Flowers

These Buddhists look like lotus flowers to me
All in one colour on the green moss
Sitting in padmasan in the water
Who are they meditating on?

All these shaven-headed Buddhist children
In Dharamshala
Look like lotus buds to me
Plants whose roots are not in the soil.

These are all descendants of that lineage of people
Who, leaving their roots behind
Migrated along with the Dalai Lama;
These people are severed from their environs
They have not brought along a patch of their sky.
What could they give to the next generations
Except tales of what their faith was!

न इनके पास फ़िज़ा है, न फ़लक, न ज़मीं
इक अनदिखी सी किसी बेल से जुड़े हैं तिब्बत से
इक अनदिखी सी किसी बेल पर महकते रहते हैं!

They have neither their culture, nor their sun,
                    nor their land
On some unseen creeper they cling to Tibet
On some unseen creeper they remain fragrant.

मेरे फ़िश टैंक में . . .!

मेरे 'फ़िश टैंक' में जो छोटी-छोटी मछलियाँ हैं
बड़ी होने लगी हैं
ख़्याल आता है क्या कोई . . .
समन्दर या कोई दरिया भी होगा,
याद में उनकी?
ये मेरे टैंक में आने से पहले भी
किसी और 'टैंक' में पैदा हुई थीं!

बड़े होने लगे हैं, टैन्टों और ख़ेमों में बच्चे . . .
कई सालों से जो 'शरणार्थी' कैम्पों में थे!

In My Fish Tank

The many small fish in my tank
Are growing up . . .
Does the thought ever come to them
The memory of a river or some sea?
Before they came to my tank
They were born in another 'tank'!

Children in tents and shelters
Who have lived in 'refugee camps' for years
Have begun to grow up . . .

कबड्डी

लकीरें हैं तो रहने दो
किसी ने रूठ कर गुस्से में शायद खींच दी थीं
उन्हीं को अब बनाओ 'पाला' और आओ—
कबड्डी खेलते हैं!

मेरे पाले में तुम आओ,
मुझे ललकारो, मेरे हाथ पर तुम हाथ मारो और भागो
तुम्हें पकड़ूं, लिपटूं, टांग खींचूं और,
तुम्हें वापस न जाने दूं

तुम्हारे 'पाले' में जब 'कुडी कुडी' करता जाऊं मैं
मुझे तुम भी पकड़ लेना
मुझे छूने नहीं देना वो सरहद की लकीरें
किसी ने गुस्से में जो खींच दी थीं!
उन्हीं को अब बनाओ 'पाला' और आओ—
कबड्डी खेलते हैं!

Kabaddi

If the border lines are there, let them be
Perhaps in anger
Someone drew them on the ground
Let's use them now as dividing lines for a game . . .
Come, let's play kabaddi!

When you cross over to my side
You challenge me, hit my hand, and run
I will catch you, grip you, pull your legs and
Prevent you from going back.

When I come over to your side saying 'kodi, kodi'
You too catch me
Don't let me touch the border line
That someone drew on the ground in anger!
Let's use them now as dividing lines for a game . . .
Come, let's play kabaddi!

लकीरें

लकीरें हाथ में थीं तो मुक़द्दर थीं
इन्हें हम बन्द रखते थे
ज़मीनों पर बिछीं तो फिर समन्दर, मुलक, घर, आंगन सभी को
काटती गुज़रीं!

लकीरें ज़िन्दा रहती हैं
लकीरें सांस लेती हैं
लकीरों पर पड़े पांव, तो पांव काट देती हैं
लकीरें रेंगती हैं
लकीरें रेंगती हैं जब तो सांपों की तरह ये केंचुली अपनी बदलती हैं।

Lines

When lines were only etched on the palm
They told our destiny
We kept them closed in a fist;
When they are drawn on the ground
They cut across oceans, countries, homes and hearths.

Lines remain alive
Lines breathe
Lines lash at feet that dare to cross them
Lines slither;
When lines slither they shed their skin
Like snakes do.

टैटू!

उसने जाने क्यों अपने दायें कन्धे पर
नील गाय का इक टैटू गुदवाया था
मर जाता कल दंगों में,
अच्छे लोग थे—
गाये देख के छोड़ दिया!

Tattoo

For no particular reason
He had the blue cow tattooed on his right shoulder
He would have been killed in the riots yesterday
But they were good people—
Seeing a cow, they let him go!

आने वाली गाड़ी . . .

आने वाली गाड़ी . . .
छः नम्बर के प्लैटफ़ॉर्म पर आयेगी—पर कह नहीं सकते
आयेगी यहीं पर, जब आयेगी—
और कुछ बूढ़े मुसाफ़िर उतरेंगे, जो इसी सफ़र में बूढ़े हुये हैं

यात्रियों के हाथ नहीं है, गाड़ी का रुकना और चलना
ड्राइवर पर निर्भर है जो 'जमुहरियत' की गाड़ी अपनी मर्ज़ी से
ड्राईव करता है!

Awaiting the Train

The expected train
Will arrive at platform number six—
But can't say though;
When it comes
It will come here
And then some old passengers
Who have grown old in this very journey
Will alight.

Passengers have no say
In the arrival or departure of the train
Depends on the driver
Who runs the locomotive of democracy
Entirely according to his whims!

सुलताना डाकू का आख़िरी ख़त–बेटे के नाम

जब तक सांस गले में थी–
तीस बरस तक, बेटा मैंने चोरी की
छीन लिया–जब चोरी करना मुश्किल था
ख़ून किया–जब छीना-झपटी मुमकिन न थी
वो भी ख़त्म हुआ तो फिर–सूली का फन्दा पहन लिया
इतने ही सालों के बाद तुम्हारी बारी आयेगी, ये याद रहे

छ: साल के बच्चे पर लाज़िम है
बाप का पेशा सीखने से आग़ाज़ करे
सियासतदान से याद रखो पंगा न लेना
उसके बच्चे पांच बरस से सीखने लगते हैं!

बशुक्रिया सुजीत सराफ़

Sultana Daku's Last Letter to His Son

My son,
As long as I had life in my lungs
For the last thirty years
I have robbed;
When robbing became difficult
I just grabbed;
When I couldn't grab or rob any more
I murdered;
When that got over
I wore the hangman's noose;
Don't forget, your turn will also come
After as many years.

It is compulsory for a six-year-old
To begin life by learning his father's profession
But remember, don't ever mess with a politician
Their children begin to learn from the age of five!

With thanks to Sujit Saraf.

कोट्टायम के क़स्बे में!

कोट्टायम के क़स्बे में
पार्टी ऑफ़िस रोज़ अपने ही नियम से खुलता है
बूढ़ा कॉमरेड मैनन अब भी बात किया करता है क्या होगा जब
इन्क़लाब आयेगा
रूस की तमसीलें देता है
इस क़स्बे के पार्टी ऑफ़िस की छत पर टांगा, या लटका
सुर्ख़ दरांती और हथोड़े वाला पर्चम
बरसों से, तूफ़ान, हवा, बारिश और धूप से लकवा खाकर
लटक गया है . . .
कितना ख़ून बहा है इसका
रंग भी अब मैनन के पान के कत्थे का सा लगता है!

In Kottayam Town

In Kottayam town
The party office opens according to its set routine
The ageing Comrade Menon still speaks about
What will happen when the revolution comes
And gives examples of the Soviet Union;
Dangling from the roof of the party office
Is a red flag of the sickle and hammer
Through decades of storms and winds and rain and sun
It has hung
As if struck by a stroke
So much of its blood has ebbed away
That even its colour now looks
Like the rusty betel juice in Menon's paan!

खिड़की का कांच!

खिड़की का कांच अब्बू की मेज़ पे बिखरा पड़ा है
कुर्सियां सोफ़े औन्धे पड़े हैं
बर्तन सारे 'सिंक' में हैं, और
पानी गिरते-गिरते फ़र्श पे बहने लगा है
स्कूल बन्द हुये हैं शायद
गर्मियों की छुट्टियों में बच्चे घर आये हैं!

आग लगी है कई जगह पर, कांच उड़े हैं
कारें सड़क पर औन्धी पड़ी हैं
धुआं हलक़ में अटक रहा है
बहते-बहते खून सड़क पर जमने लगा है

मन्दिर मस्जिद बन्द हैं शायद,
गर्मियों की छुट्टियां हैं!

Broken Window

The glass from the broken window
Is scattered across Father's table
Chairs and sofas lie upside down
Dishes remain unwashed in the sink
And the overflowing water is all over the floor;
Perhaps, the schools have closed for summer
And the children have come home.

Many streets are on fire, broken glass is all around
Cars lie upside down on the road
Smoke chokes the throat
The flowing blood has begun to congeal on the street
Temples and mosques are closed;
Perhaps the summer holidays have begun!

सड़क से रक़्स करते . . .

सड़क से रक़्स करते, गुल मचाते दंगे गुज़रे हैं
रिपब्लिक-डे पे जैसे झाँकी जाती है
बड़े खुश थे, जलाते थे अलाव जब बसों के,
और घेरा डाल कर नारे लगाते थे!
किसी के चेहरे पर न ग़म, न ग़ुस्सा
यही लगता था वर्ल्ड कप जीत कर, इक टीम लौटी है!

Procession

Like some pageant in the Republic Day parade
The rioters dance on the road,
Celebrating.
They are very happy turning buses into bonfires
Jumping around them, shouting slogans.
Their faces show neither sorrow nor anger
It seems
A team has returned after winning the World Cup.

अयोध्या

बड़ा छोटा शहर है अब, जहां का रहने वाला था
फ़लक पर धूप की मान्निद जो अब फैला हुआ है
उसी की 'जन्मभूमि' देखने आया, अयोध्या में
सलाख़ों में घिरा है, आहनी जंगलों के पीछे छोड़ कर
सुनता है लोगों की . . .
कृतार अन्दर कृतार आते हैं मिलने
ज़्यादा पास जायें तो
सिपाही पहरे पर, बन्दूक़ से पीछे हटा देते हैं लोगों को
कभी 'अवतार' था वो—
सरासर इक मिनिस्टर लग रहा है आजकल का
'सुरक्षा' के बिना हिलता नहीं वो!

Ayodhya

Where he once lived
Is a very small town now;
Now he is spread across the sky
Like the light of the sun;
I came to Ayodhya to see his 'janmabhoomi'.

Surrounded by iron bars
He sits behind strong barricades
Listening to people now . . .
Hordes of people come to see him;
If you go too close
The sentry on duty
Pushes the crowd back with his gun.
He was an *avatar* once—
But looks completely like a minister today
Not moving an inch without security!

मुहाफ़िज़!

मुहाफ़िज़ हूं मैं अपनी सरहदों का
कोई मेरी ज़मीं पर पाँव रखे तो, मैं उसको भून देता हूं
मैं अपनी सर-ज़मीं का पासबां हूं
अगर दुशमन कोई गोली चलाये तो
मेरे सीने से गुज़रेगी तो पार होगी वो सरहद से
मैं उस गोली को अपने देश की मिट्टी पे गिरने भी नहीं दूंगा!

मेरी सरकार मुझको . . . इसलिये . . .
टैक्स सारे कट कटा के
दस हज़ार और तीन सौ पैंतीस रूपये हर माह देती है।

The Protector

I am the protector of my country's borders
If somebody lays a foot on my land
I riddle him with bullets;
I am the sentinel of my beloved country
If the enemy fires a bullet
It must pass through my chest to cross the border;
I will not let that bullet touch the soil of my country!

For this, my government
After deducting all taxes
Pays me
Ten thousand three hundred and thirty-five rupees
Every month!

एक मंज़र!

ये मंज़र पहले देखा है!
फ़ौज की फ़ौज खड़ी है जम कर
बन्दूकें ताने कन्धों पर
और हुजूम इक लोगों का, बाहें लहराता
शायद उन्नीस सौ उन्नीस, और अमृतसर है
जलियानवाला बाग़ से मिलता जुलता है

या उन्नीस सौ छत्तीस में लाहौर का मंज़र
तहरीके आज़ादी के उस सालाना जलसे का दिन है

इस मंज़र में कितना कुछ जाना पहचाना सा लगता है
इन लोगों के चेहरे भी पहचाने से हैं
इन चेहरों पर मायूसी और गुस्से की तहरीरें भी
उनकी उम्रें, उनके जज़्बे
मैं उन सब से वाक़िफ़ हूं

हो सकता है, सन् उन्नीस सौ बयालीस था और इलाहाबाद था
चौक के बीचों-बीच बने इस गोल जज़ीरे के जंगले में

I Have Seen This Scene Before

I have seen this scene before!
A whole army standing entrenched
With guns on shoulders, ready to fire
And, in front, a crowd of people
Waving hands;
Perhaps it is 1919, and Amritsar
Somewhat like Jallianwala Bagh.

Or maybe it is the scene of Lahore in 1936:
The day of the freedom struggle's annual assembly.

So much in this scene seems to be familiar
The faces appear to be known
The despondency and anger on their faces
Their ages, their emotions
All of this, I am acquainted with.

Maybe, it is 1942 in Allahabad:
In a railed-off island
In the centre of the town square

फ़ौज की फ़ौज खड़ी थी जम कर
दायरा खींचे, बन्दूक़ें ताने कन्धों पर
और हुजूम इक लोगों का, बाहें लहराता
बल्ली-बल्ली हाथ उछलते हुये हवा में, मुट्ठियां भींचे
लोगों के हाथों में तब भी
ऐसा ही इक झन्डा था
नारों की आवाज़ यही थी
इसी तरह से चली थी गोली
इसी तरह कुछ लोग गिरे थे
इसी सड़क पर खून बहा था

चौक के बीचों-बीच मगर, इस लोहे के जंगले के अन्दर
इक अंग्रेज़ का बुत था पहले
अब गांधी की मूर्ति है

लेकिन अब तो . . .
सन् उन्नीस सौ बानवे है!

An entire army in readiness
Lines drawn, their guns ready to fire
And in front a mob of people
Waving hands;
Their fists clenched
The same flag in their hands
The same slogans on their lips
The bullets fired in the same way
Some people dying as they died before
Blood flowing the same way on this very street.

But, in the railed-off island
In the centre of the square
The statue then was of an Englishman
Today, it is a statue of Gandhi . . .

But now . . .
Now the year is 1992!

युधिष्टर

लाख के घर में—
पाँच थे वो, एक उनकी गायिका थी
पास के गांव से उन सबको बुलाया था, युधिष्टर ने
लोकगीत, संगीत सब सुनते रहे
सोने के टुकड़े दिए थे—
सोमरस भी इस क़दर उनको पिलाया था कि सारे सो गये!

रात के अन्धेरे में फिर पांचों पांडव
ख़ुफ़िया रस्तों से निकल कर चल दिये
मुड़ के भी देखा हो शायद . . .
लाख का पूरा महल जब जल गया
और ढेर होकर गिर गया—

कौरवों को छः के छः शव मिल गये
कितनी दूरअन्देशी थी! युधिष्टर की!

Yudhishtir

In that house of lac
They were five, and a female singer
Yudhishtir had invited all of them
From the neighbouring village;
There was music and singing
Pieces of gold were given as gifts
And plenty of wine . . .
They all fell asleep.

In the darkness of the night
The five Pandavas then left
Through a secret tunnel;
They might have turned back to see
The entire palace of lac burning
Falling in a heap to the ground.

The Kauravas found all six bodies;
How prescient Yudhishtir was!

यस! युधिष्टर—
हाँ! सियासत में यही होता है, अब भी
एक राजा बिना,
परजा का हर शख़्स सिर्फ़ इक हिंदसा है
लिख लिया, जब जी किया
जी किया जब धो दिया!

महाशेवता देवी की नज़र।

Yes, Yudhishtir—
Yes! This is what happens in politics even now;
Except for the king
Each of his subjects is but a number:
Written down when desired
Erased when not required!

For Mahashweta Devi.

बड़े बूढ़ों की टोली बैंच पर . . .

बड़े बूढ़ों की टोली बैंच पर बैठी हुई . . .
हर रोज़ जब अख़बार पढ़ती है . . .
हवाला आज का लेकर
सभी पिछले दिनों की बात करते हैं
'तुम्हें तो याद होगा, *"राम पंजवानी"*—
ये लाठीचार्ज की तस्वीरें देखीं—?
तुम्हें लगता है क्या अंग्रेज़ वापस जा चुके हैं?'

किसी की कार गुज़री आगे पीछे चार जीपें साइरन देती हुई
'गुप्ता जी' ने दांत गिरने से संभाले और हंसे
'क्यों? क्या कोई अंग्रेज़ पीछे रह गया क्या?'
'नहीं *राने मिनिस्टर* जौगिंग करने जा रहे हैं पार्क में!'

'छगन' आये तो बोलेः
'अरे साहब कभी सोचा था क्या पीने का पानी भी बिकेगा बोतलों में?

Old Men on Benches

A bunch of old men sitting on benches . . .
Every day when they read the newspaper
They speak of days gone by
Giving the reference of today:
'You would remember, Ram Panjwani—
Have you seen these pictures of a lathi charge?
Do you feel the English have actually left?'

Someone's car passes by
With four jeeps going along, blaring sirens;
Guptaji, holding on to his dentures, laughs:
'What? Has some Englishman been left behind?'
'No, Minister Rane is going for a jog in the park.'

When Chhagan comes, he says:
'Did you ever think, my friends, that drinking water
Will be sold in bottles?

कहीं भी रुक के पी लेते थे ''पियाओ'' पर
हमेशा गर्मियों में ठंडे कपड़ों में लपेटे मटके लग जाते थे बाग़ों में!'

ना जाने कौन से वक़्तों की बातें करते हैं बूढ़े!

'*मियां मन्नान*' आते हैं तो थोड़ी देर उर्दू बोल कर जी हलका करते हैं
कि बलग़म की तरह अब फेफड़ों में जम गई है

गणेशी 'गायेत्री' पढ़ते हुये आते हैं
मन्दिर से,
ख़रीद कर लाए हैं 'पुड़िया'
उठा के चुटकियों से वो तिलक देते हैं, कहते हैं
'हमें तो भस्म भी अब नक़ली लगती है!'

We would stop whenever we felt thirsty
At the *piyao*
And earthen pots of water wrapped in wet cloth
Used to be kept in the park in summer.'

God alone knows what times these old men talk about!

When Miya Mannan comes
He talks in Urdu for a while
To lighten his heart;
The language, like phlegm
Has by now congealed in his lungs.

Ganeshi walks in chanting the Gayatri mantra;
He has come from the temple
Where he has bought a small packet of ash
He lifts a pinch for each one and makes a *tilak*, saying:
'I think now even the holy ash is adulterated!'

तिड़का कप!

तिड़का कप के जैसा था वो
उसका हैन्डल था ही नहीं!

कोई मुंह न लगाता था, लब जल जाते थे
हाथ में लो तो, गर्म था, उंगलियां जलती थीं
'बॉस' ने इक दिन बाहर फेंक दिया उसको
'चल साला दलित!'
सब के चहरे तिड़क गये हैं दफ़्तर में!

A Cracked Cup

He was like a cracked cup
There was no handle to him.

No one would put it to the mouth
For the lips would burn;
It was hot, if held in the hands
The fingers would get scalded.

One day the boss threw it out:
'Get out you Dalit!'
Now there is a crack on every face in the office.

आदमी हल को खींचते हैं तो . . .!

बैलों की जगह, जब आदमी हल को खींचते हैं तो
सींग निकल आते हैं उनके
बोझ से गर्दन झूलने लगती है, जब उसको
पैर की पांचों उंगलियों से
खुश्क ज़मीं को पकड़-पकड़ के पांव उठाने पड़ते हैं
ऐड़ियां फट जाती हैं उसकी
बैलों के खुर जैसे बीच से फटते हैं!

नाल लगाना बाक़ी है, वरना ये आदमी
ज़मींदार के चाबुक खाके चलने वाले चौपाये से कम है क्या!

The Human Plough

Instead of oxen, when a man has to pull a plough
He grows horns
His neck begins to droop with the weight
Using all five toes of each foot
He tries to grasp, step by step, the dry earth
His heels split
Just like the hooves of oxen
They are riven down the middle.

A *naal* needs to be put on him . . .
Otherwise how is this man
Any different from the four-legged creature
That moves when the landlord cracks his whip?

मकोड़ा!

दीवार पे लटके चाकू की जिस धार पे एक मकोड़ा
इतनी देर से ऊपर नीचे टहल रहा है
उस चाकू से मौसम्बी काटी थी किसी ने
बार-बार कुछ चाटता है उस धार पे और फिर
सामने वाले पैर उठा कर सूंघता है

कितनी बार गिरा और संभला
रस तो सूख चुका है कब का
धार पे जीभ कटाने में अब रस आता है
यार मेरे को—!

उसका अंत मुझे मालूम है, वो भी जानता होगा मेरा
हम दोनों को तेज़ धार पे कट के उतरना होगा!
हम दोनों दलित हैं!

The Ant

A large ant has for long been strolling up and down
On the edge of a knife hanging from the wall
It was used by someone to cut a sweet lime
The ant repeatedly licks something on the knife's edge
And then lifts his front legs to smell them.

How many times has he fallen and recovered his balance?
The juice has dried long ago
Now the flavour comes
When the tongue is cut by the blade.

I know what his end will be
And he knows mine, probably
Both of us can descend from the razor's edge
Only after we are slashed.
Both of us are Dalits!

लौटते पानियों से . . .

सारा दिन मैं कैरल के लौटते पानियों में जब कश्ती खेता हूँ
छान-छान कर नारियल के पत्तों से किरणें, मेरे बदन को सैंकती हैं
सीली हवा, नमकीन समन्दर से उठकर
तेल सने बालों में उंगलियाँ फेरती है!

रात गये घर लौटता हूं जब . . .
चूल्हे में गोबर के उपले जलते हैं तो, उनका धुँआ,
मेरे बदन के पोरों में भर जाता है!

सांस खींच के मेरे बदन की खुशबू—
सूंघो, देखो, दलित के नंगे बदन से कैसे
ज़िंदगी की ख़ूशबू आती है!

From the Backwaters

When all day I row the boat
In the backwaters of Kerala
The sun's rays
Sieved through the coconut trees
Warm my body
The moist air rising from the salty sea
Runs its fingers through my oil-drenched hair.

Late at night when I return home
The smoke from the dung cakes in the fire
Suffuses the pores of my body.

Take a deep breath
And smell the scent of my body
See, how from the naked body of a Dalit
Rises the fragrance of life!

हाई हील्ज़!

ऊँचे जूते पहना करो, ऐ दोस्त हमेशा
क़द में मुझसे छोटे हो तुम
और ऊपर देख के एक दलित से बातें करते
तुमको हमेशा झेंप आती है
माथे पर चुन्नट डालने से तुम और सुकड़ जाते हो!

ऊँचे जूते पहना करो तुम, ऊँची ज़ात से हो!

High Heels

Wear shoes with high heels, my friend
Your height is less than mine
And you always feel a little awkward
When you have to look up and talk to a Dalit;
The crease that forms on your brow
Only shrivels you further!

You must always wear shoes with high heels
You are from a high caste!

ब्लड टैस्ट!

शीशी भर के ख़ून की, वो ले गये हैं
क़तरा-क़तरा खोल कर देखेंगे क्या बीमारियां हैं

इक दलित की मुफ़लिसी, विरसे में आई है, मेरे ख़ूं
में मिलेगी
ताबेदारी हुक्मरानों की, जो मेरे आबा-व-अजदाद में थी
और ग़ुलामी भी तो कुछ पुश्तों तलक
ख़ून में रह जाती है

थोड़ी सी गर्मी है ख़ूं में
पर कोई विस्फोट का ख़तरा नहीं
छोटे-छोटे से जेरासिम
अब, बग़ावत के, भी शामिल हो गये हैं
वो नज़र आते नहीं हैं आंख से
ख़ूर्दबीं के नीचे रख कर देखने पड़ते हैं वो

हां, 'अना' की किरकिरी शायद मिले!

Ego—'अना'

Blood Test

They have taken my blood
To examine, drop by drop, all the ailments.

They will find a Dalit's poverty
Part of my inheritance;
The loyalty to overlords
That was there in my ancestors
Slavery too for some generations
Leaves its traces in the blood.

There is some hot-bloodedness
But no danger of explosion;
Some small germs of rebellion
Have now made their entry
They cannot be seen by the naked eye
You have to use a microscope to perceive them.

Yes, perhaps
You may find some irritating grains of 'ego'!

बॉर्डर की चौकी!

वो एक चौकी जड़ी हुई है जो बॉर्डर पर
उसी की दीवार में जड़ा एक सिपाही राईफ़ल लिये खड़ा है
जमाहइयाँ ले रहा है कब से
उसे भी अब नींद आ रही है
वो थक गया है

लकीर अपनी जगह से हिलती नहीं, न हटता है सिपाही
छपे हुए लफ़्ज़ की तरह से पड़े हैं दोनों।

न जाने कल रात क्या हुआ था
गले पे बन्दूक़ रखके उसने
चला दी गोली।

वो लफ़्ज़ लेकिन मरा नहीं है
वहीं पे राईफ़ल लिये हुए दूसरा सिपाही जड़ा हुआ है!

Border Post

In the checkpost embedded in the border
Is embedded a soldier standing with his rifle
Yawning since how long . . .
Even he is sleepy by now
And tired.

The line of the border does not move
Nor does the soldier
Like the printed word
Both are fixed where they are.

God knows what happened last night:
He put the gun to his neck
And fired a bullet.

The word, however, has not died;
At the same spot is embedded now
Another soldier with a rifle.

कराची!

तेरे शहर में भी तो चीलें
उसी तरह लाशों के ऊपर मंडलाती हैं
जैसे मेरे शहर के चौराहों पर
बन्दोबस्त की गोलियां खाकर . . .
लोगों की लाशें जब गिरती हैं
आसमान पर मंडलाते गिद्ध नीचे उतर आते हैं।

हम दोनों के, दो मुल्कों में
आम आदमी कितने मिलते जुलते हैं!

Karachi

In your town too
Vultures hover above corpses
In the same way as in mine;
When in town squares
The dead fall hit by *bandobast* bullets
The vultures come swooping down.

You and I . . .
In the two countries to which you and I belong
The common man looks so similar!

पड़ोसी

जब तक मेरे सामने वाले घर में रौशनी जलती है
मेरे कमरे की दीवार पे
उस घर की परछाईयाँ चलती रहती हैं

इक 'व्हीलचेयर' है
धक्का खा के दाऐं-बाऐं घूमती रहती है
उस घर की दो पालतू चिड़ियां उड़ती हैं तो मेरी इस दीवार से टकरा जाती हैं
उस घर में लटका इक पिंजरा, मेरे घर का पिंजरा लगता है

जाने कौन सी खिड़की बन्द होती है, जिसकी जाली से
दीवार पे जेल का दरवाज़ा बन जाता है
आते जाते लोग सभी क़ैदी लगते हैं

नंगा लटका बल्ब कभी हिल जाए तो
लोग हवा में उड़ने लगते हैं
इक सर्कस लग जाती है
कुछ देर ग़दर मच जाता है

Neighbours

So long as the light is on in the house opposite
Its shadows keep moving
On the wall of my house.

There is a wheelchair
Pushed around left and right;
Two birds, kept as pets
Hit my wall as they fly about
The cage that hangs in that house
Looks like the cage of my house.

Some window closes, and its grill
Forms prison bars on my wall
All those who pass by look like prisoners.

If the naked bulb hanging on a wire swings sometimes
People start swaying about in the wind
Just like a circus act
A tumult goes on for a while.

फिर वो खिड़की खुल जाती है
और कोई बत्ती जलती है
दो झूमते साऐ लिपटे-लिपटे, बालकनी में, आके खड़े हो जाते हैं
शायद मेरे घर की जानिब देख रहे हैं

कभी-कभी यूं भी होता है
उस घर के धूऐं की परछाई, मेरी दीवार पे पड़ती है
तब लगता है . . .
दोनों घरों में आग लगी है!

The window opens again
Another light comes on
Two swaying shadows, entwined with each other
Come and stand on the balcony;
Perhaps they are looking towards my house.

Sometimes it so happens
The shadow of the smoke in the house opposite
Falls on the wall of my house—
And it seems as if both houses are on fire!

सरहद पर ये सक्ता क्यों है?

सरहद पर ये सक्ता क्यों है?
इस बर्फ़ाब सी ख़ामोशी से डर लगता है!

बगुले जैसी ख़ामोशी मक्कार बहुत है
एक टांग पर खड़े-खड़े भी
एक आँख से ध्यान लगाये
दूजी आँख खुली रखती है

जब भी कोई हलचल हो तो
सरहद की दोनों जानिब ही
कांटेदार आवाज़ों के कुछ केकट्स उगने लगते हैं!

सरहद के रेगिस्तानों में,
सांस दबा कर चलती है ख़ामोश हवा
रेत, ज़मीं से गर्दन घिस कर उड़ती है

सरहद पर सक्ता तारी है
सरहद की बर्फ़ाब सी इस ख़ामोशी से अब डर लगता है!

Still Border

Why is the border so still?
One feels afraid of the frozen silence.

This silence is very deceptive:
It stands on one leg like a heron
One eye is in meditation
While the other remains watchful.

At the slightest movement
On either side of the border
The cacti of voices begin to sprout.

In the desert along the border
The wind hushes its voice
The sandflies creeping along the ground.

The border continues to be still
One feels afraid of the frozen silence!

मन्जर (छब्बीस जनवरी)

बड़ी ठन्डी हवा थी, और छब्बीस जनवरी थी!
फ़िज़ा में कुहरा था, लाहौर था . . .
दरया-ऐ-रावी बह रहा था . . .
कचहरी बंद थी, और छत पे अंग्रेज़ों का झन्डा था
वो तीनों दम-बखुद दीवार से लग के खड़े थे
सुबह की दूर से सांसें सुनाई दे रही थी
उन्हें उस रात छत पे चढ़ के अंग्रेज़ों का वो परचम गिराना था
वो तीनों सोच कर आये थे हिन्दूस्तान की पोशाक बदलेंगे!
ज़फ़र बल्लम पे था, जब सर में यूं जाकर फटी गोली कि
पूरे मुलक में छींटे पड़े उड़ कर . . .!

बड़ी ठन्डी हवा थी, और छब्बीस जनवरी है
फ़िज़ा में कुहरा है,
दिल्ली में 'झांकी' चल रही है
लाहौर में दरया-ऐ-रावी बह रहा है!

26th January: A Scene

The wind was bitingly cold, and it was 26th January
Fog was all around, and it was Lahore
The river Ravi was flowing . . .
The *kachehri* was closed and on its roof was the British flag
Those three stood silently, their bodies stuck to the wall
The dawn was quite distant still
But they could hear the breath of the morning
That night they would climb to the roof
And bring down the British flag
The three of them had resolved to change the attire of India!

Zafar was on the pole when the bullet exploded in his
head
The drops of blood flew across the country.

The wind is bitingly cold, and it is 26th January
Fog is all around
The celebration is on in Delhi
In Lahore the river Ravi is flowing . . .

ज़फ़र के साथ वो पर्चम गिरा तो था . . .
लहोर और दिल्ली के पर्चम अलग हैं अब!

With reference to Bela Lal's novel.

That flag did fall along with Zafar—
But now the flags in Delhi and Lahore are different!

With reference to Bela Lal's novel.

आंखों को वीज़ा नहीं लगता!

आंखों को वीज़ा नहीं लगता
सपनों की सरहद होती नहीं
बन्द आंखों से रोज़ मैं सरहद पार चला जाता हूं,
मिलने 'मेहदी हसन' से!

सुनता हूं उनकी आवाज़ को चोट लगी है
और ग़ज़ल ख़ामोश है सामने बैठी हुई है
कांप रहे हैं होंठ ग़ज़ल के!
जब कहते हैं . . .
'सूख गये हैं फूल किताबों में
यार "फ़राज़" भी बिछड़ गये हैं, अब शायद मिलें वो ख़्वाबों में!'
बन्द आंखों से अक्सर सरहद पार चला जाता हूं मैं!

आंखों को वीज़ा नहीं लगता
सपनों की सरहद, कोई नहीं!

Eyes Don't Need a Visa

Eyes don't need a visa
Dreams have no frontiers
Every day, with eyes closed, I go across the border
To meet Mehdi Hassan!

I hear that his voice is wounded
And the ghazal sits silently before him
Its lips tremble
When he says:
'The flowers inside the book have dried
Dear Faraz has also parted
Now, perhaps, we can meet
In dreams only . . .'

With eyes closed I often go across the border.
Eyes don't need a visa
Dreams have no frontiers.

रमज़ान के दिन थे!

सुनो, इस बार भी रमज़ान के दिन थे,
मैं पाकिस्तान आया था . . .
मेरे 'वीज़ा' में 'इफ़्तारी' तलक रुकने की गुंजाईश न थी
मैं बॉम्बे लौट आया।

कराची के समन्दर पे मैं इक काग़ज़ की कश्ती रखके आया हूं
हवा का रुख़ कभी बदला तो शायद बह के आ जाये
वगरना चांद निकला ईद का जिस दिन,
उसी को फूंक से तुम मेरी जानिब ठेल देना
मैं साहिल पर खड़ा हूं
मैं साहिल पर मिलूंगा!

Days of Ramzan

This time too, in the days of Ramzan
I was in Pakistan . . .
My visa didn't stretch till Iftar
I returned to Mumbai.

I placed a paper boat on the sea at Karachi
If the direction of the wind changes
It may sail towards me;
Otherwise, when the Eid moon appears
Blow on it
And push it towards me
I am standing by the sea
You will find me at the shore.